DATE DUE

Grover's Day at the Beach

A Counting Story

By Jessie Smith
Illustrated by Tom Cooke

Featuring Jim Henson's Sesame Street Muppets

A Sesame Street / Golden Press Book
Published by Western Publishing Company, Inc., in
conjunction with Children's Television Workshop.

ISBN: 0-307-13105-X / ISBN: 0-307-63105-2 (lib. bdg.)   A B C D E F G H I J K L M

One day Grover Monster went to the beach with his friends. They started to build a sand castle. Grover went down to the water's edge with his pail. "I will get some water for the moat," he said.

Grover spotted something blue and shiny in the
wet sand.

"Oh, my goodness!" he said. "What have we
here?"

He picked up an old bottle with a cork in the top.
Then he noticed that there was something inside it.

"Hey, everybodee!" called Grover. "Look what I
found!"

Grover's friends ran over to see.

"There's a message in the bottle, Grover!" said Betty Lou. "What does it say?"

Grover tugged and tugged on the cork. Finally it popped out of the bottle, and Grover pulled out a piece of paper.

"Today you will count to twelve," Grover read.
"Oh, my goodness! All the way up to twelve!
I wonder what to count first."
"You can start with the bottle," said Betty Lou.
"Right!" cried Grover. "One wonderful bottle!"

Two inflatable sea horses bobbed in the water by the shore.

"Ernie and Bert must have parked their sea horses here until they are ready to go paddling," said Grover. "Meanwhile, I will count them!

"Two cute and adorable inflatable sea horses!

2

"Oh, dear," said Grover. "What shall I count now?"

"How about the waves, Grover?" asked the Count. "I love to count waves!"

Grover looked out at the waves crashing in on the shore.

"That is it, Count!" cried Grover.

"I see three wonderful waves!"

It was a very busy day at the beach, and a very
sunny one, too.

"I know!" said Grover. "I will count the colorful
beach umbrellas. I see four.

"Four beach umbrellas."

4

Grover clumped on down the beach.

"Hey! I caught something!" Oscar The Grouch yelled from the pier. "And what a great catch!"

"What is it, Oscar?" called Grover. Then he saw.

"Oh, well. I guess I can count five old shoes.

5

"Oh, dear," said Grover. "Whatever will I count now?"

"I have it, Grover!" said the Count. "Sailboats! I love to count sailboats."

Grover looked out to sea. He spied six sailboats with white sails.

"Six beautiful sailboats!" he counted happily.

On the way back to the unfinished sand castle,
Grover looked up.

"Oh, look!" he cried. "Somebody is flying kites for
me to count.

"Seven glorious kites.

"Pant, pant!" said Grover when he got back to the sand castle. "Counting is very hard work! What will I count next?"

"How about sea gulls?" suggested the Count. "I love to count sea gulls."

High above their heads eight graceful sea gulls swooped and soared.

"Of course!" cried Grover. "Sea gulls. I will count them.

"Eight elegant sea gulls.

8

"We have important work to do besides counting," said Grover. "We must finish building the sand castle."

Cookie Monster happened by. He was eating a Popsicle.

"SLURP!" said Cookie. He ate up his Popsicle. Then he gave the stick to Grover, along with the other sticks in his fist.

"Oh, thank you, Cookie Monster!" said Grover. "I will make a Popsicle-stick fence for my sand castle.

"Nine Popsicle sticks."

Bert wanted to help, too.

"Here, Grover," he said. "These Figgy Fizz bottle caps are the finest from my collection. Would you like to use them? They would be keen on the sand castle!"

Grover and Bert carefully placed the bottle caps as windows all around the sand castle.

"Ten Figgy Fizz bottle caps!" Grover counted. "Terrific!"

10

"I found these shells on the beach, Grover," said Ernie. "Do you want them for the sand castle?"

"I am so lucky to have such thoughtful friends!" cried Grover. They put the seashells on the sand castle, one by one.

"Hmm…" said the Count. "I love to count seashells."

"Eleven super seashells!" said Grover.

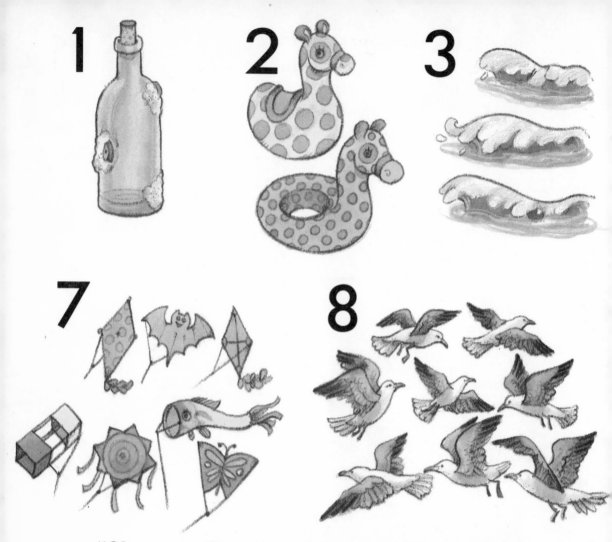

"Oh, my goodness!" said Grover. "The message in the bottle said that I would count up to twelve today."

Grover counted again all the things he had seen. He counted one bottle, two inflatable sea horses, three waves, four beach umbrellas, five old shoes, six sailboats, seven kites, eight sea gulls, nine Popsicle sticks, ten bottle caps, and eleven seashells.

4

5

6

9

10

11

"Oh, dear!" said Grover.
"I have only counted to eleven.

"What am I going to do?" said Grover. "Maybe my friends will help me."

"Friends!" cried the Count. "I love to count friends."

"That is it!" said Grover. "I will count my friends. One, two, three, four, five, six, seven, eight, nine, ten, eleven friends...and me! That makes twelve wonderful friends. Terrific!

12

"Oh, I am so happy!" said Grover. "I counted all the way up to twelve at the beach today."

"But you didn't count grains of sand, Grover!" said the Count. "I love to count grains of sand."